Shouke

By Naoko Ikeda

ISBN 978-1-4950-1930-2

WILLIS MUSIC

EXCLUSIVELY DISTRIBUTED BY

HAL•LEONARD®
CORPORATION
7777 W. BLUEMOUND RD. P.O. BOX 13819 MILWAUKEE, WI 53213

Visit Hal Leonard Online at
www.halleonard.com

From the Composer

The general theme of *Shoukei* is summer. A perfect summer's day may start with an early morning bike ride ("Bicycling" in **C Major**; note the upcoming circle of 5ths). In mid-morning, wander through a flower field ("Little Lavender" in **G Major**). Then, take a walk and a skip on a silvery beach ("Beachside Step" in **D Major**) before spending the evening relaxing in the harbor listening to distant Latin sounds from a passing yacht ("Habanera" in **A Major**). The pieces in the key of A Minor introduce traditional Japanese elements.

When I wrote these pieces a decade ago, I envisioned a sunny summer's day in Japan. But I know that this perfect day could happen anywhere in the world.

Naoko Ikeda

February 2015

Performance Notes

Little Lavender (G Major)
Imagine walking through fields of lavender. Play gently.

Moon Flute (A Minor)
"Taketori Story" (or, The Tale of the Bamboo Cutter) is one of the oldest Japanese tales from the early Heian Era (10th century). A little baby girl, Kaguya, is found in the forest and brought up lovingly by a childless bamboo cutter and his wife. She grows up to be beautiful and wise. But on the night of a crescent moon, a moon flute plays mournfully, informing her she is actually a princess and must return to the moon and bid farewell to her friends and family forever. (This is a sister piece to "The Silver Boat," found in *Celestial Dreams*, published in 2007.)

Sakura (A Minor)
Cherry blossoms (*sakura*) symbolize the Japanese Spring. Imagine floating flower petals and play expressively.

Beachside Step (D Major)
Skip happily on the burning sand. Be particularly aware of the left hand position, and count the rests correctly.

Habanera (A Major)
It's a hot summer night and there is music coming from a brightly-lit yacht in the harbor. The same habanera rhythm should sound different from the one in "Beachside Step."

Bicycling (C Major)
You are on a bicycle riding up and over rolling hills. What kind of scenery do you see?

...You (F Major)
I wanted the melody and harmony to be reminiscent of an American ballade from the 1980s. The sixteenth notes should be played as if speaking to someone special. Please choose a word that comes before "you."

Contents

Sakura

by Naoko Ikeda

Under the cherry trees in full bloom

In softly swinging sunlight

Fiercely swaying to the right

Alone.

I will remember

…the joy of seeing you again

…to speak out loud, as in my dreams

…our dance, huge on a movie screen

Under the cherry trees in full bloom

I am alone

I won't forget

My promise.

With thanks for translation assistance from Takako Teranishi and Charmaine Siagian.

Little Lavender

Naoko Ikeda

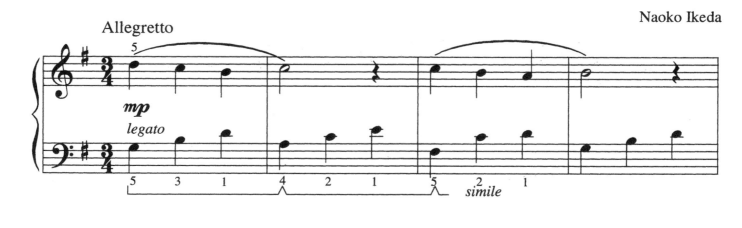

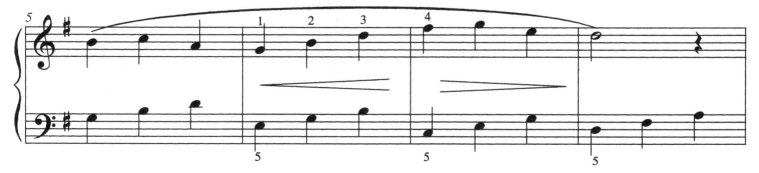

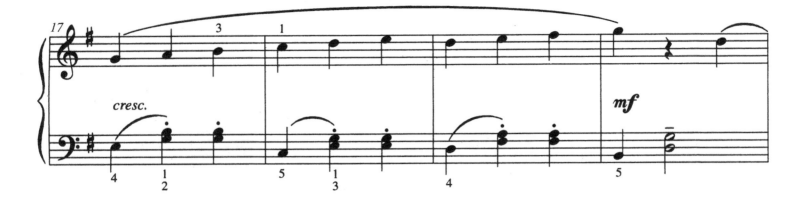

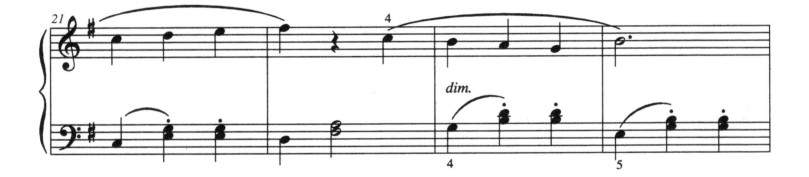

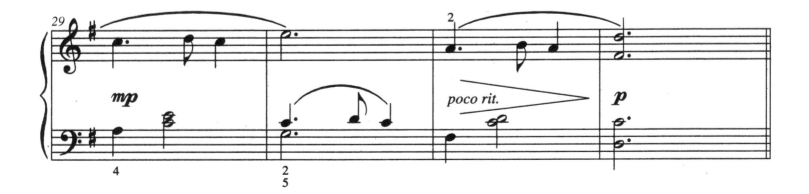

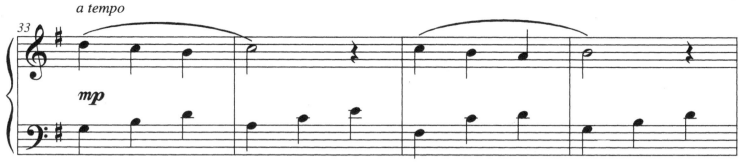

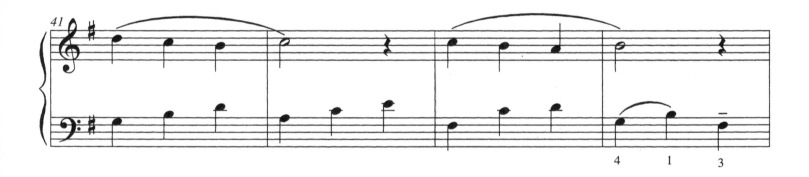

To Tomoko Tutui

Moon Flute

Naoko Ikeda

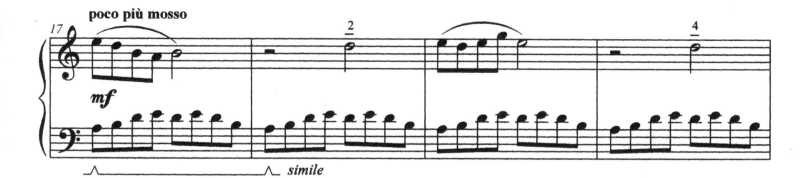

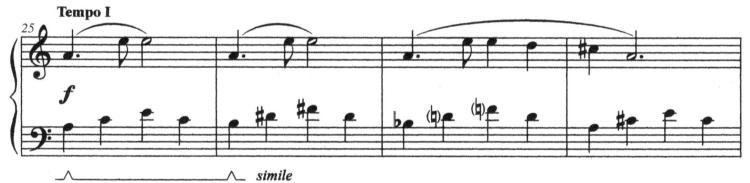

Sakura

Naoko Ikeda

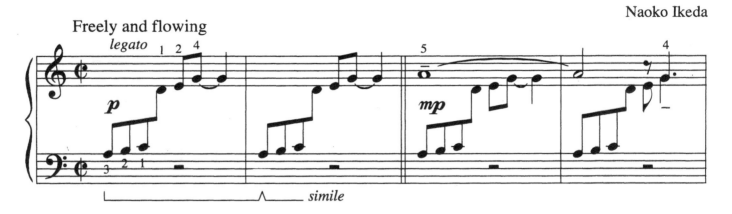

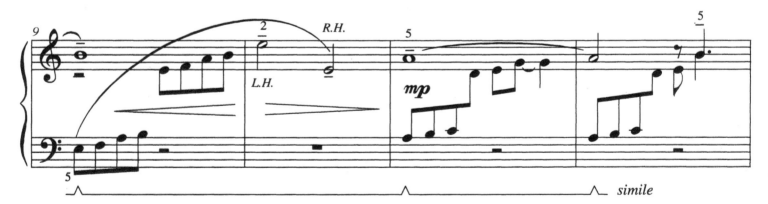

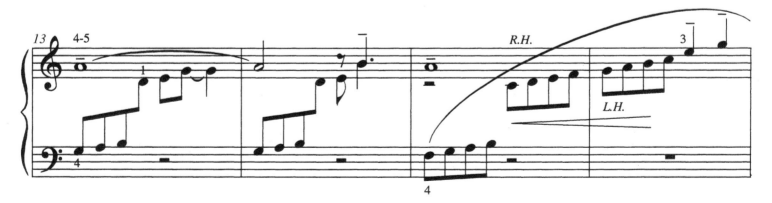

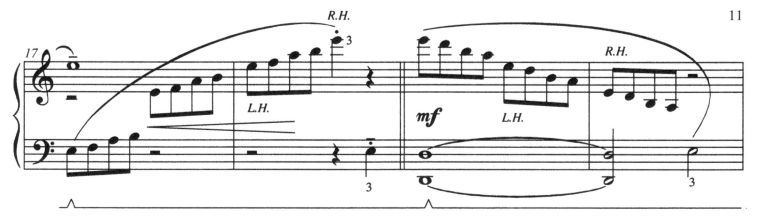

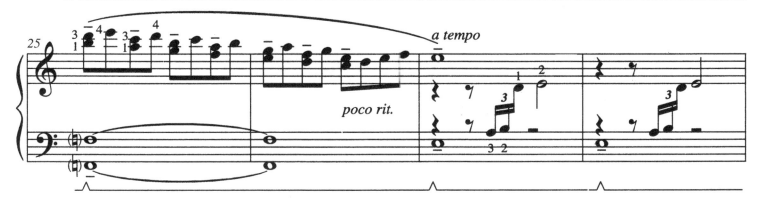

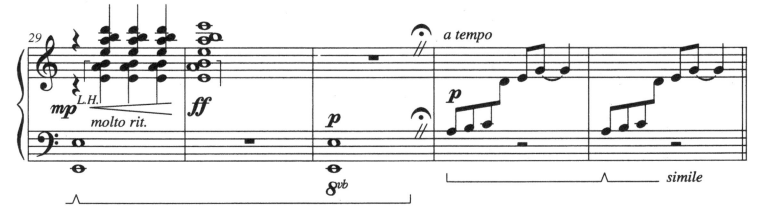

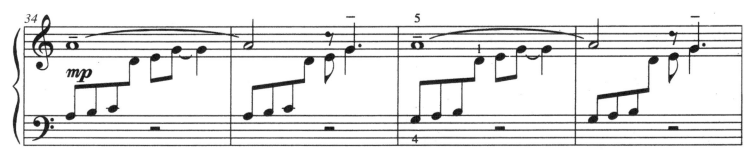

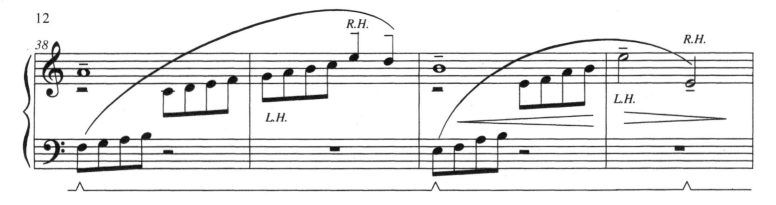

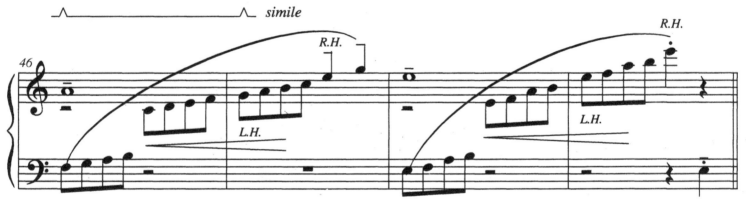

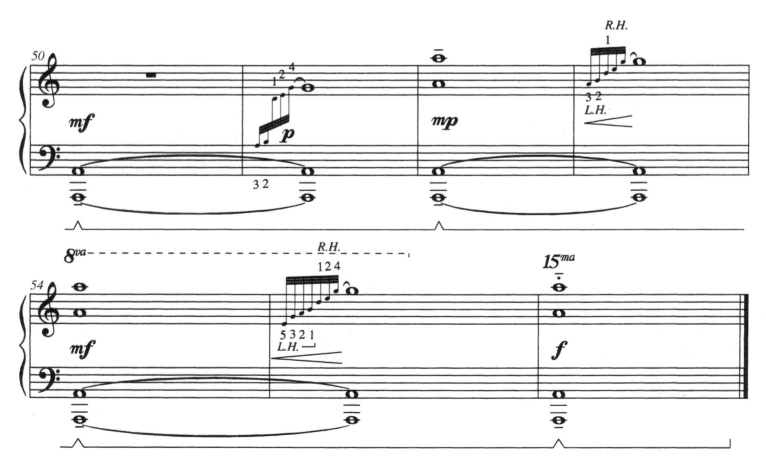

To Yoshi-Nori

Beachside Step

Allegro con spirito

Naoko Ikeda

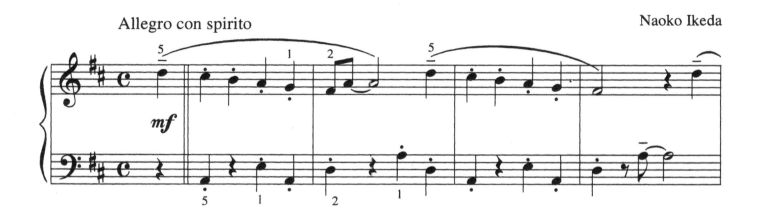

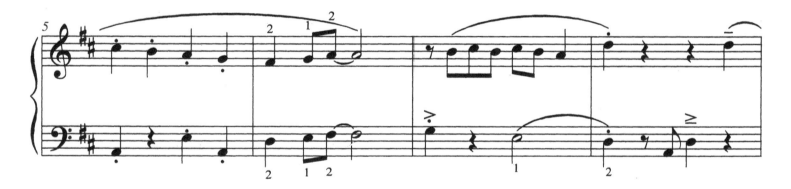

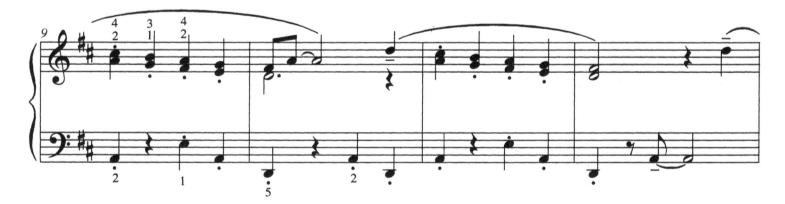

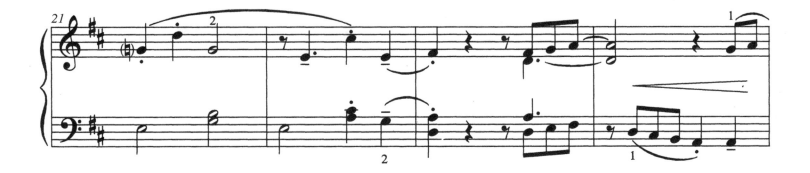

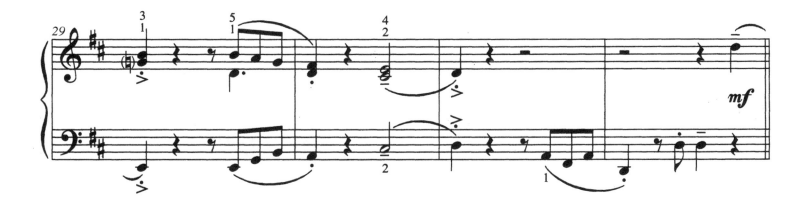

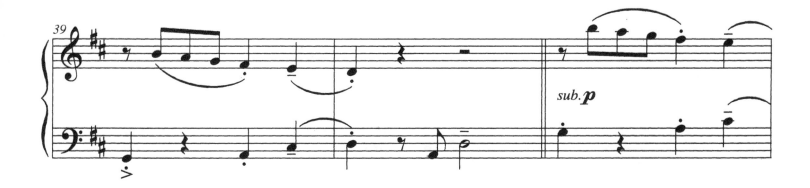

To my friend Noriko

Habanera

Naoko Ikeda

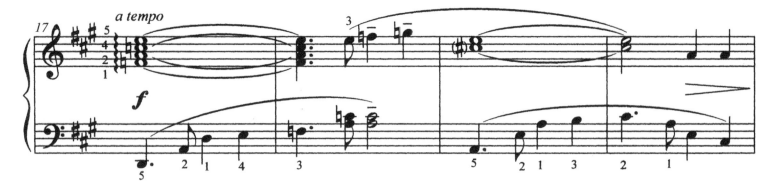

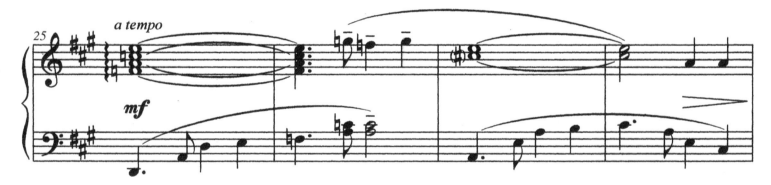

To Takako Teranishi

Bicycling

Allegretto

Naoko Ikeda

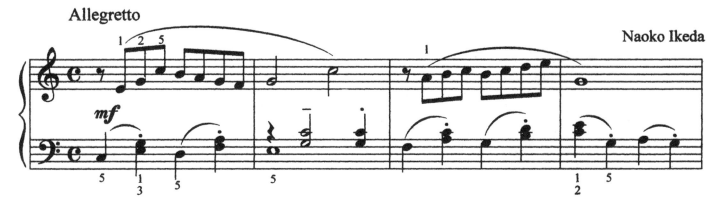

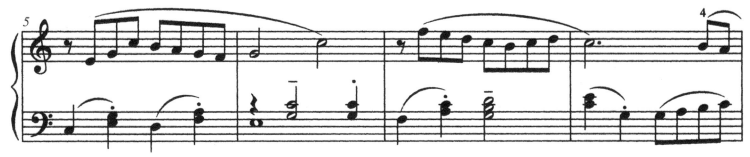

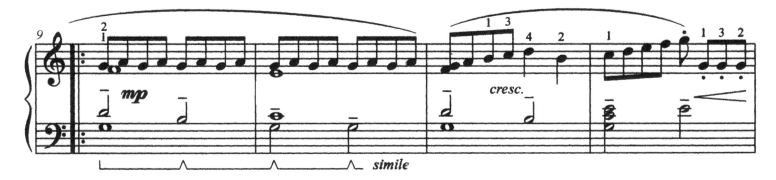

...You

Naoko Ikeda

Medium ballad

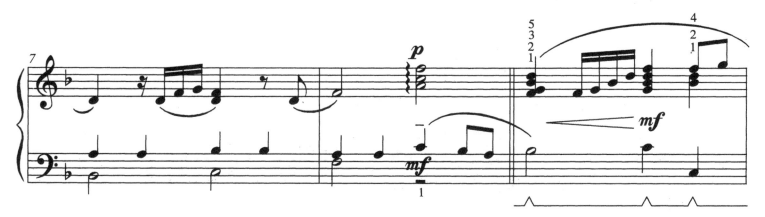

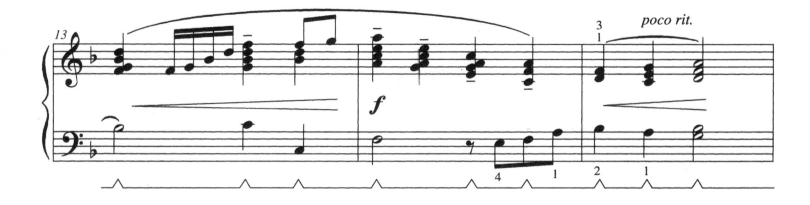

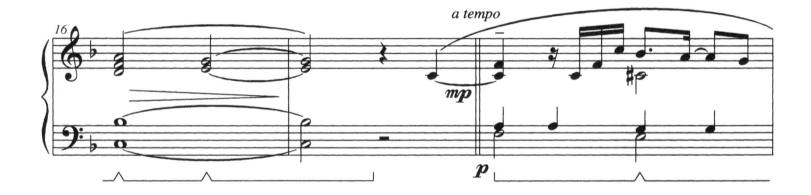

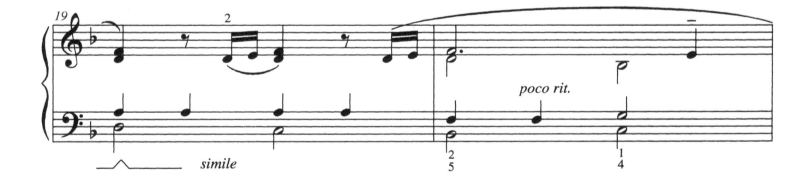

CLASSIC PIANO REPERTOIRE

The *Classic Piano Repertoire* series includes popular as well as lesser-known pieces from a select group of composers out of the Willis piano archives. Every piece has been newly engraved and edited with the aim to preserve each composer's original intent and musical purpose.

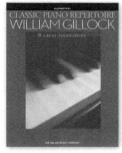

WILLIAM GILLOCK – ELEMENTARY
8 Great Piano Solos
Dance in Ancient Style • Little Flower Girl of Paris • On a Paris Boulevard • Rocking Chair Blues • Sliding in the Snow • Spooky Footsteps • A Stately Sarabande • Stormy Weather.
00416957 ....$8.99

EDNA MAE BURNAM – ELEMENTARY
8 Great Piano Solos
The Clock That Stopped • The Friendly Spider • A Haunted House • New Shoes • The Ride of Paul Revere • The Singing Cello • The Singing Mermaid • Two Birds in a Tree.
00110228 ....$8.99

JOHN THOMPSON – ELEMENTARY
9 Great Piano Solos
Captain Kidd • Drowsy Moon • Dutch Dance • Forest Dawn • Humoresque • Southern Shuffle • Tiptoe • Toy Ships • Up in the Air.
00111968 ....$8.99

LYNN FREEMAN OLSON – EARLY TO LATER ELEMENTARY
14 Great Piano Solos
Caravan • Carillon • Come Out! Come Out! (Wherever You Are) • Halloween Dance • Johnny, Get Your Hair Cut! • Jumping the Hurdles • Monkey on a Stick • Peter the Pumpkin Eater • Pony Running Free • Silent Shadows • The Sunshine Song • Tall Pagoda • Tubas and Trumpets • Winter's Chocolatier.
00294722 ....$9.99

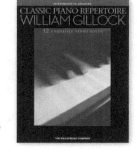

WILLIAM GILLOCK – INTERMEDIATE TO ADVANCED
12 Exquisite Piano Solos
Classic Carnival • Etude in A Major (The Coral Sea) • Etude in E Minor • Etude in G Major (Toboggan Ride) • Festive Piece • A Memory of Vienna • Nocturne • Polynesian Nocturne • Sonatina in Classic Style • Sonatine • Sunset • Valse Etude.
00416912 ....$12.99

EDNA MAE BURNAM – INTERMEDIATE TO ADVANCED
13 Memorable Piano Solos
Butterfly Time • Echoes of Gypsies • Hawaiian Leis • Jubilee! • Longing for Scotland • Lovely Senorita • The Mighty Amazon River • Rumbling Rumba • The Singing Fountain • Song of the Prairie • Storm in the Night • Tempo Tarantelle • The White Cliffs of Dover.
00110229 ....$12.99

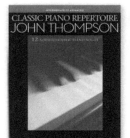

JOHN THOMPSON – INTERMEDIATE TO ADVANCED
12 Masterful Piano Solos
Andantino (from Concerto in D Minor) • The Coquette • The Faun • The Juggler • Lagoon • Lofty Peaks • Nocturne • Rhapsody Hongroise • Scherzando in G Major • Tango Carioca • Valse Burlesque • Valse Chromatique.
00111969 ....$12.99

LYNN FREEMAN OLSON – EARLY TO MID-INTERMEDIATE
13 Distinctive Piano Solos
Band Wagon • Brazilian Holiday • Cloud Paintings • Fanfare • The Flying Ship • Heroic Event • In 1492 • Italian Street Singer • Mexican Serenade • Pageant Dance • Rather Blue • Theme and Variations • Whirlwind.
00294720 ....$9.99

WILLIS MUSIC

EXCLUSIVELY DISTRIBUTED BY
HAL•LEONARD®

CLOSER LOOK View sample pages and hear audio excerpts online at **www.halleonard.com**

www.willispianomusic.com

www.facebook.com/willispianomusic

Prices, content, and availability subject to change without notice.

Composer **Naoko Ikeda** grew up and still resides in the beautiful city of Sapporo in northern Japan. Influenced by classical music, jazz and pop, as well as the piano works of William Gillock, her own music reflects her diverse tastes with beauty, elegance and humor. Ms. Ikeda is a proud graduate of the Hokusei Gakuen school system, and holds a piano performance degree from Yamaguchi College of Arts. She maintains an energetic schedule as teacher, clinician, and composer.